FROM DREAM
TO REALITY

DREAM TO REALITY RESOURCES

There is a growing online support structure of materials and social media hangouts all geared toward supporting dream builders. It's important to get plugged in and stay connected so that you have support when the path gets rocky and rough. Visit the empowerment website to access D2R- focused blogs and online chats. There is also an Empowerment Tribe group page on Facebook, as well as a closed *From Dream to Reality* Facebook group for those working through this book.

Would you like to start your own D2R *(Dream to Reality)* support group? Imagine the power of bringing local like-minded dream builders together for idea exchanges and creative strategy sessions. Head over to UBeEmpowered.com to learn more.

FOLLOW JANETTE R. SMITH
JanetteSmith.com   UBeEmpowered.com

PERISCOPE
@JanetteRSmith

FACEBOOK
@Janette.R.Smith/facebook
https://www.facebook.com/groups/1603564546551500/

TWITTER
@JanetteRSmith   #DreamBelieveBuild

INSTAGRAM
@Janette_sWorld

FROM DREAM TO REALITY

Navigating the Path to Your Life Purpose

Janette R. Smith

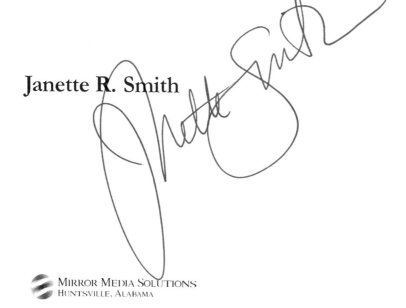

MIRROR MEDIA SOLUTIONS
HUNTSVILLE, ALABAMA

FROM DREAM TO REALITY

Navigating the Path
To Your Life Purpose

Copyright © 2015 by Mirror Media Solutions Publishing
ISBN- 978-0-692-55081-6

Printed in USA Mirror Media Solutions

DEDICATION

This is for my fellow dreamers and empowerment tribe members
who push daily to find and fulfill their calling and purpose.

I offer special thanks
and limitless heartfelt gratitude
to the Creator and Giver
of all dreams...
We did it again!

ACKNOWLEDGMENTS

An infinite amount of love goes to
Marc, for inspiring the writer in me,
Mommy, *(Eva P.)* my favorite girl,
who never stopped believing and
Daddy, *(Lt. Col. (ret) John E. Smith)*
whose love, wisdom and wit
continue to guide me.

To my Dream Builder family
Patrick, Sheri, Joya and P2—
thank you for "holding up my arms"
with your support, faith, laughter
and love.

...a future with hope.

CONTENTS

INTRODUCTION

$\mathcal{L}$ike most children, dreaming came quite naturally to me. Since I was an only child for six years, I spent quite a bit of time creating and living in imaginary worlds. Being a dreamer at such an early age is quite acceptable and often encouraged.

Around the age of three I began showing signs of being performance oriented. Translation: I was a ham. My parents wisely directed me and that "ham" energy into music lessons at the Yamaha School of Music in Colorado Springs, Colorado. It was there they discovered that I also had a passion for talking. At the age of seven I would write poetry and create books. By the time I was in fifth grade, I was typing scripts for my own original plays inspired by movies I'd seen. My parents would tell the story about the summers I'd spend banging away on my grandmother's old, mechanical Remington typewriter. After a few days I'd emerge with a script for my play, which included colorful carbon copies for all the members of the cast.

I held auditions in my driveway. The talent pool was the neighborhood kids. I can't tell you how I managed to get them to show up every day at 3:00 p.m. for non-paying rehearsals with no promise of an actual performance.

If you would have asked me what I wanted to be when I grew up, I would have said a singer or actor. While I've enjoyed some measure of development and success in those areas, it has been clear that my calling was based in other talents and skills that reflected my greater strengths and deeper purpose: writing, producing, directing, video editing, public speaking, and communications. Now when I think back on my youth, I see I was also developing my natural abilities to encourage, inspire, lead, motivate and entertain.

Over forty years later, I can honestly say I have used all of those skills and natural gifts in very meaningful and powerful ways. Everyone has the seed of a dream sown inside them, but as we grow older we're told to "get real" when we begin to explore the desires of our heart. However, it is within the process of dreaming that we find the keys to our true purpose and calling.

To have a dream is only the beginning. To fulfill that dream takes courage, tenacity and a tremendous amount of faith. "How will I make this happen?" The answer to that question is revealed progressively. The journey from dream to reality can take many paths and is largely dependent upon the decisions and actions of you—the dreamer. *How* is discovered from one level of learning to the next, like pieces of the puzzle. The revelation of *how* is also earned through perseverance, which is why many dreamers are left stranded on the shores of desire, believing their dream is an unattainable goal. However, for those who are passionate, courageous and driven, this is the beginning of a wondrous adventure.

This book is the culmination of research, experience, and shared advice from all the great dreamers I have interviewed over 25 plus years as an award-winning journalist and entertainment host. From Oprah Winfrey to Hugh Grant, Spike Lee to Zig Ziglar, and many other great artists and thought leaders, I was intrigued by the backstory of how they built their dreams. Though they vary, I took the strategies they used and created the path of *how* for me. Following that path, I have been able to identify my purpose for each season of life, reposition from one level of success to the next, reposition, dream and build again. Each time I have taken on the dream building process I have enjoyed true fulfillment and, yes, financial gain.

Likewise, your life purpose is *your* great assignment. It solves a problem in the world, and that service holds value. Each dream I ever reached for has become a reality. This book itself is a dream fulfilled.

My great passion has always been to help others realize their dreams. So, as you read the following pages, give yourself permission to hope and remove any limits on this self-excavation and dream building process. Make room for inspiration so you can learn how to tune into your inner wisdom, set purpose-driven goals, and navigate your own unique path from dream to reality.

DESTINY -
MORE THAN A DECISION

The word "destiny" is scary for some people. It shouldn't be. Destiny is just another form of the term destination. Your destiny is a deliberate place you set to reach. That's where your life purpose takes you. Whether you like it or not we're all going to end up somewhere. Don't you want to make sure you've made every effort to have a say in where you end up?

Most of us would say we want to live a life that's fulfilling on all levels: personal, professional, spiritual, physical, and material. But, if you randomly ask people if they are happy with their lives, very few say "yes." There are numerous reasons for that disconnect. Some people have chosen not to pursue their purpose because of their own fear or the fear of others, so they're left with a void of unsettledness. Others begin to pursue their purpose but give up during the process— not willing to weather the challenges that come along. Still, others are actually successful in their vocations; but sadly, their jobs have little to do with their life's great purpose. At some point in their lives they decided to become someone chosen for them or to do work they had little passion for in exchange for greater social acceptance or financial gain. Finding and fulfilling your purpose isn't just a decision; it's a discovery process. If you're reading this book, you may have become disillusioned with your current job or the promotion you've been working toward. Perhaps, you have lost your job or several jobs over the last few years or are now repositioning into a new life stage unable to push past "stuck." Maybe you started a family and put your dreams on hold before you could really pursue your purpose and calling. No matter the reason, by investing in reading and working through this book, I imagine you are hungry to define or recommit to your dream and ignite or recapture the passion that comes from creating a life of great purpose.

I remember the season in my life when passion and purpose moved to the forefront in my pursuit of happiness. I was in my early 30's, no longer enamored with the success of "living the dream" of a very successful news anchor. I was working in a top ten market, living in a trendy uptown apartment condo, hanging out with a great group of "notables," and going to work daily in designer clothes. Every morning I'd get up thinking, "This job is so much fun. I better make it look a little more tedious or the 'powers that be' may catch on and quit paying me." Still, something in me was hungry for more. If you're thinking I must have been ungrateful, I would say you weren't completely wrong. Looking back I was grateful, because I knew there were hundreds of people who would have loved to have my job and lifestyle. Yet, I had to admit that through the years the sense of purpose, the drive, passion and even the principles that made me want to be a journalist had somehow started fading.

Growing up, I didn't dream of being a journalist. In fact, I barely watched the news as a teenager. I just didn't find it engaging at all, nor could I relate to the great news men of that time (Sorry Mr. Cronkite). I respected them and their authoritative swagger. I just didn't see myself in them, or a part of the *news* industry. In college, I had no idea what to major in. I was still not sure what I wanted to be.

By this time I had spent fourteen years studying classical piano and taking voice lessons. My parents made it clear I would need a "real job" after graduation, so pursuing a music major was dismissed. The only thing I knew to do was follow my passion. Talking, writing and creative thinking skills landed me in the Telecommunications department where television production and performance courses were offered.

I had chosen a major but still had no real sense of purpose. I was still caught up in the dream of singing or being a performer of some sort. When a high school friend, who was as close to me as a little brother, landed a role on broadway - my heart leaped for joy! At the same time, I felt a pinch of sadness. I had helped him grow in many ways. Now he was on the big stage while I considered myself to be stuck in college and far from my dreams. In a bold move I decided to run off to NYC. My parents found out and assisted me with my plan, putting some parameters around the trip. I didn't care. I was going to NYC and make my dreams come true. When I got there, I was moved by the creative energy of the city and my friend's work ethic. I went with him to commercial auditions and auditions for tv pilots, but I just didn't seem to connect in that world. I wanted to be on broadway too; I wanted to act and perform. I decided to go and pursue this dream, but I just didn't seem to fit. Again, discovering your purpose isn't about what you think you aspire to or about what others accomplish. It's not even about a decision to follow a path. Your purpose is aligned with your unique assignment in this life. It's more than a decision - it's a discovery.

The powerful thing about pursuing your purpose is that while you are on the path toward *it*, your purpose is actively working to get to you. I left NYC having enjoyed the learning experience, but more certain that being on broadway wasn't what I should be focused on. I returned to Alabama A&M University. Even though I didn't know how I would use my skills, what I wanted to become or what role a major in Telecommunications would play in my life, I surrendered to the idea of getting the degree and building my natural talents and interests. Just being in the right place on the path to purpose positioned me closer to my dreams, dreams I hadn't even fully solidified in my own mind.

In the fall of 1987 a news crew from WAFF-48 NBC in Huntsville, Alabama, was on the campus of Alabama A&M University doing a story. While other students were not interested in being interviewed, the "ham" in me was MORE than happy to oblige, so I did the interview. When the station's news director, Pat Brown, saw the footage, he asked the reporter Wes Torain to get in touch with me because he thought I had a strong "on camera" presence. Remember, I wasn't very interested in the new business and was even less interested in this job when I found out it was a secretary's position. I met with Mr. Brown, and that's when things started coming into focus. He talked about the news industry's purpose and how local news stations served our communities. He explained how each role in the station fit into that purpose. Mr. Brown told me that journalists were mirrors to the world and emphasized the responsibility and character it took to reflect truth to the public. In that interview Pat (as I would later call him) never asked how many words per minute I could type. He spent over an hour casting vision that enabled me to see I was created to be a part of this powerful industry. Soon after, I was hired as a newsroom secretary, a paid position that also allowed me to earn college credit for my necessary intern work. I had found where I fit. Through years of mentoring by news directors Bob Morford, Garry Kelly and numerous production crew members I developed and excelled. Eight years later I left WAFF 48 as the second African-American prime time anchor in the Huntsville/Decatur/Shoals market which served north Alabama and southern Tennessee.

Twelve years later, the news seemed to be evolving from the trusted source for facts and unbiased presentations. Newscasts were now referred to as "shows," and they were becoming showy with more entertainment and personal opinions sprinkled in. Even decisions about some of our content was being influenced by advertisers and sponsors. It wasn't enough to be a journalist anymore; celebrity factories are what some stations seemed to become. Ever so slowly the industry was changing. I was changing too. Little did I know the "something more" I hungered for would lead me down the path of building my next dream. That dream would completely redirect my life's path.

In 2000, while working at WFAA-TV in Dallas, Texas, I developed pneumonia and and became very ill. It almost proved fatal. I had emergency surgery, was moved to ICU, and then endured a thirty day recovery stay in the hospital. You might imagine that an aha moment was born out of this medical emergency, but that's not quite what happened. When I left the hospital I was most grateful for a full recovery. Though I didn't know what was wrong, something was definitely not right. Oddly, when I returned home I was strongly compelled to relocate. I somehow "knew" I was supposed to move to Atlanta. When I shared this with my mother she asked, "What are you going to do there?" "I guess more of what I'm already doing?" I answered. I really had no clue. I just knew I was supposed to move. I trusted my *inner knowing,* so I started packing.

In the process of preparing to move, I began reading *The Path* by Laurie Beth Jones. This book rocked me off what I thought was a firm foundation. It walked me through creating a mission statement for my life. I came up with E.I.E.I.O. I wanted to **Encourage, Inspire, Entertain and Inform people in Original ways.** Now that was an aha moment for me, because it pinpointed why I had wanted to be a journalist in the first place. It also shed light on why I no longer felt I was living out that purpose. When I held this new banner up against my career, there were many areas that weren't measuring up.

This became more evident in the days following 9-11. I was a News Anchor in Atlanta, Georgia, at the time. We were actually on the air when the planes struck the twin towers. Like most news agencies, we were reporting 24 hours a day following the tragedy. Often we saw and heard things too disturbing to air. When the country slowed down and seemed to be getting its rhythm back, I asked myself why I still felt so lost and disconnected. I was immersed in every aspect of the stories of recovery, attending producer meetings to give input and to suggest stories that would help heal, encourage and inspire our communities during the strain of recovering from troubled times. Wasn't this living under the E.I.E.I.O. banner? I could not answer "yes." I had no real drive fueling me. Something in me was beginning to shut down. I wasn't the only person experiencing these feelings. I remember talking to former CNN anchor Bobby Batista and CNN producer David Bernknopf years later. They left CNN within the year following the 9-11 attack. The tragedy caused them to do some self-inspection as well, and they started a successful media consulting business together.

When it came to changing careers in pursuit of my purpose and passion, the process didn't happen as quickly for me as it did for my colleagues. I hung on for as long as I could pretending everything was fine and that I was still fulfilled doing news because I felt I should have been. I was later reminded by my most wise inner voice,

"Making change is never as difficult as accepting change." Change came. I wasn't thrilled about it at the time, but the end of my contract with that station cleared the way for me to accept greater career opportunities, enjoy financial gain and experience meaningful spiritual growth. I had to be we willing to give up the great for something greater. I did. As a result, I was able to gain more personal freedom and become more fulfilled in every day living. I let go of what wasn't great enough and stepped out with faith and a plan to pursue much more.

I have built several dreams over the years. I went from student to journalist and from entertainment host to media ministry director. From there I joined the ranks of small business owners and consultants and later became a certified life strategist and mindset coach. Throughout the process, I remained an ardent student of the successful journeys of men and women on the path to something greater.

For me, it all started after I read one small book that asked one big question, "What is your mission statement for life?" Over the course of reading this book, I'm going to ask you some weighty questions; and, as I sit typing, I'm excited just thinking about what wonderful changes will take place in your own life as a result of discovering those answers.

From Dream to Reality

We are all creative beings. Think about it. We imagine, we think, we plan, we build. The Wright Brothers looked up to the sky and entertained the idea that they could create an apparatus that would enable humans to fly like birds. They had absolutely no proof that this was true. Their only inspirations were the musings and studies of Leonardo Di Vinci and a flying toy their father once gave them, made of bamboo and cork—it was powered by rubber bands. This may seem rather insignificant, but this toy planted a seed that encouraged them. That encouragement cultivated their thinking, igniting an idea, which fueled a dream and initiated a plan that was further developed through research and testing, ultimately producing a pilotless kite.

You thought I was going to say, "Our first 'flying machine.' " Nope. The Wright Brothers' quest for success was a decade-long obsessive pursuit of testing, failing and doing it all again. Sound familiar? With just that brief summary of their inspiring story, you should begin to understand that there is no magical formula for birthing a dream. There is no drive-through pick up window for purpose. The process is more of a journey that takes you from one level of completion to the next.

It will test:

- the motives behind your dream

- your capacity to step out on faith

- your willingness to work for it

- the character needed to attain and maintain it.

Understanding these points is crucial to the process of navigating your path from dream to reality because it helps distinguish between the dream that is rooted in your life's purpose and a dream created from ego or fascination. You must also determine if something you feel compelled to pursue is a calling (a purpose-driven urge toward a particular way of life or career) or a cause (a principle, or movement you are drawn to defend because of a deep passion). A calling serves your highest purpose, and though you may walk out that call through various vocations in numerous ways, your calling remains steady.

For instance, Oprah Winfrey has a call, I believe, to educate, inform and entertain. She shares in her book *What I Know For Sure* that, "Using my voice as a force for good: It's what I was meant to do."[1] Her call drove her to change formats of her television talk show from confrontational to connectional. In moving from TV show host to network CEO, the vehicle she's used to support that calling has changed, but her purpose has remained the same.

A cause on the other hand is driven by your passion, and it may change focus several times throughout your life. You may be driven, for instance, to support cancer research and work diligently with organizations charged with fund-raising for that cause. You may also feel passionately about protecting the earth and environment. In addition, you may choose to help out a family member by babysitting the little ones while he or she goes to back to school or take on a volunteer position at your church. You may feel compelled to assist a neighbor or friend as a caretaker. For some these may be a calling, but for others, these are causes. Your great dream which births your life purpose transcends a cause.

"We grow great by dreams. All big men are dreamers. They see things in the soft haze of a spring day or in the red fire of a long winter's evening. Some of us let these great dreams die, but others nourish and protect them; nurse them through bad days till they bring them to the sunshine and light which comes always to those who sincerely hope that their dreams will come true."

~ Woodrow Wilson

Notice that the 28th American President mentions "nourishing and protecting" dreams so that they can reach "sunshine and light." The terminology paints an image of planting and cultivating something—a seed.

Your dream is a "seed." The seed is invaluable, but it becomes useless if it is never given an opportunity to produce the thing it was created to. If you want an apple, you don't eat the seed pretending it's an apple. You plant the seed in good soil, nurture and protect it; and, in due time, it produces an apple-bearing tree. Though dreams are intangible, they hold the same power as any other seed that brings forth a form of life.

Your Dream is a Seed

Dreams are also extremely important because they instill confidence and hope in the dreamer. They offer what I call "Faith Photos"—*mental pictures to help propel us toward our dream through conviction and inspiration.* This is most important as you go through the difficult seasons that will come. I find it helpful to journal or keep a data folder of voice recordings about my current dream. At any time I can go back, reading through or listening to those inspired thoughts, and let the thoughts bolster my faith and reenergize my drive. If you don't believe in your own dream or work to nourish and protect it from attacks of negativity, that seed (your dream) could die or simply remain a seed.

When you connect with your dream, you'll be tempted to share it with the world. Don't! The first lesson in protecting your seed is understanding that not everyone will share your enthusiasm or even believe in your potential to fulfill it. This can be tremendously damaging to you in the early stages. Their negative words and criticism can destroy or damage the seed of your dream and replace it with seeds of doubt and unbelief. There will be a time and place to share the enthusiasm for your aspirations. Wait.

"The key to realizing a dream is to focus not on success but significance – and then even the small steps and little victories along your path will take on greater meaning."

~*Oprah Winfrey*

Significance—this is something we all yearn for. Now that we've discussed the role and importance of dreams, many of you may be left asking, "Why am I here? What is my Dream?" It's perfectly fine if you're not sure. This book is specifically designed to help clarify that.

In the next chapter we will walk through the process of determining your purpose-aimed, passion-fueled goals for this season. "This season?" Yes. Don't be alarmed by the term "season." Dreams will illuminate your purpose, but you may find that you walk it out very differently in various stages and cycles of your life.

Oprah Winfrey has worked in television for over 30 years. Though she first started using these talents as a reporter and anchor in the news industry, Oprah slowly transitioned into the entertainment industry. Ultimately, she earned her own show, which she ended after a 25-year run. Though Oprah is no longer hosting a daily talk show, she has tremendous presence and even greater influence in the broadcasting industry having shifted her focus to producing television content with corresponding live events for her new network, aptly named OWN. Oprah is the same woman, still fulfilling her dream to serve people by giving them the tools to live their best life. Instead of doing that as a talk show host, she is simply using a different platform and using other skills and talents than those of a talk show host.

So you see, a season can be short or long, but what matters most is that, at every turn along the path to purpose, you are exactly where you are supposed to be—doing exactly what you are supposed to be doing. Going from dream to reality is not an easy undertaking. Otherwise, we'd all be "living the dream."

Now, let's focus our mindset. Receive these "path agreements" as a type of contract you are making with yourself. Let's agree that you:

- will not focus on success.
- will not be ruled by fear.
- will not focus on failure.
- will focus on the process.
- will not judge yourself.
- will believe in yourself.

This is my personal mantra, feel free to use it.

DREAM . BELIEVE . BUILD .

Anatomy of
a Dream

"There are two great days in a person's life — the day we are born and the day we discover why."

~ William Barclay

$\mathcal{I}$ personally believe God gives everyone a dream that, if fulfilled, will meet a specific need and solve problems for others. This is why you may often hear the word *calling* used to define what we've been referring to as our *life's dream*. A calling is your assignment, driven by purpose, revealed to you in a dream.

If you believe there's a power greater than yourself then you must also believe that Power — which I acknowledge as God — sees the big picture down here on earth. He knew we would need doctors, firefighters, superb mothers, teachers, poets, musicians, artists and architects. So, when He decided what color your eyes would be, your hair color and height, he also placed an assignment on the inside of you. It's "seed" — your dream.

Consider a real "seed." An apple seed looks different than a watermelon seed. There are no instructions attached to either seed on what to do, how to grow or even what to be. It is what it is. The instructions in each seed's internal genetics dictate that each produces a very specific fruit. What we also know about seeds is that you have to plant it in good soil and nurture it with the necessary resources. Eventually, it will grow and produce something very specific. The same is true with that "seed" on the inside of you. And, unfortunately like a real seed, if you don't get planted, rooted, grounded and nurtured, the seed (dream) can die.

Survey your friends, and you'll find that everyone has a unique set of talents, interests and skills. We didn't pick what we ended up with (or else I would have Beyoncé's singing voice.) From the time we began growing and learning, we were also discovering or uncovering our identities. Just as the planted seed begins to reveal clues about what it will grow into, your dream (seed) begins to bring your life's purpose into focus. It's important to pursue this path and walk into your purpose because you are someone's solution. There is a question in the world that only you can answer. You are unique. You are necessary.

Sometimes we lose connection with our dream. This happens for various reasons: life's demands can pull us off track, or we form wrong assessments about our ability to achieve our dream based on damaging misconceptions.

Here are some common sentiments. Do you share these beliefs?

- Dreams are logical and realistic.
- Dreams are attached to stardom.

- Dreams unfold on their own.
- I'm not qualified to pursue my dream.

- Divinely inspired dreams come with step-by-step instructions.
- It's too late to follow my dream.

- Dreams are designed to serve my personal needs, wants and desires.

Any one of these beliefs can mislead, overwhelm, or trap you in a web of confusion. As a result, doubt may prevent you from ever beginning the journey from dream to reality. This line of thinking also produces acts of self-sabotage which initiate the Dream Destruction Cycle. I'll share more on that later. First, let's address these statements for clarity.

Dreams should be logical and realistic. Not always. Sometimes dreams will stretch the boundaries of what you believe possible for yourself. That was the case for Keith Harrell. Once a tall, skinny, awkward kid, he overcame his stuttering to become an internationally revered motivational speaker and leadership coach for corporate America. Every dream will test your level of faith, will be something you can't achieve in your own strength and will probably have aspects to it that make no logical sense to you, though it makes complete sense in the big picture from a world view. Most people are overwhelmed by the thought of their dream and would probably call it unrealistic. So, relax—you're right where you're supposed to be.

Dreams unfold on their own. Though it is a dream, you have to "wake up" to make it come true. Fulfilling it is a process that requires your avid pursuit. "Taking a wait and see approach, only leaves you standing around looking," as we used to say. If I'm in Atlanta, Georgia, and decide I want to visit my mom in Huntsville, Alabama, I can't just stare at the route on a map and expect to be magically transported there. I have to make the journey.

Divinely inspired or authentic dreams come with step-by-step instructions. Hardly! This one thing I learned first-hand and from interviewing a variety of thought leaders and influential icons of our time. *How* doesn't start showing up until you fully commit to the dream and embrace it in your heart. Once you begin formulating an action plan and walking it out, the next piece of the puzzle tends to show up. If you think *how* just falls in your lap - you will never realize your dream.

Taylor Swift took the journey from dream to reality. She dreamt of being a country music star, so she learned how to play a twelve string guitar at the age of twelve. She then coaxed her parents into letting her visit Nashville where she passed out demos of her singing karaoke songs to the local record labels. Afterwards, she began performing at a few open mic nights and started working collaboratively with Nashville songwriters in hopes of meeting the "someone" who held the next piece of her dream puzzle. For Swift, that would be Scott Borchetta, another dreamer who was working to get his newly-formed record label (Big Machine Records) off of the ground. Get it? Don't wait for *how*. Commit and follow the dream doing what you can with what you have, and the rest of the *how* will come.

Dreams are a vehicle to meet my personal needs, wants and desires. Your fulfillment will come from living out what you're most passionate about, but a true dream (calling) is not self-centered. It's about you being in service to others with a focus on contributing to your community and world by sharing your gift. Again, you're meeting needs and solving problems.

Every Dream is attached to stardom. Yes and no. When you are operating fully in your gifts and talents, you will shine. Your stage will be whatever platform you are called to work on in your immediate world. Some people do have a purpose that places them on the world's stage, but this does not in any way make that dreamer more special than any another. In truth, many of the people who deserve stars on the Hollywood Walk of Fame go sorely unnoticed. They are the mothers, fathers, teachers, doctors, small business owners, construction workers, volunteers and others who work diligently in the trenches and behind the scenes empowering others to change the world.

I'm not qualified to pursue my dream. No one is ever fully "qualified" at the point the dream is revealed. Preparation is what the journey is all about. You can also rest assured: the bigger your dream, the more challenging your journey. The challenges create opportunities for you to sharpen your tools and fine-tune your skills along the way.

I often dreamt of having positive and powerful influence with people and would see myself speaking in front of crowds. That was my dream, and I would not negotiate the possibility of attaining that goal — not even with myself. My vision became my E.I.E.I.O philosophy. In the beginning I wasn't sure how that would manifest in terms of a career. It makes sense now when I see how my life unfolded: During all my twenty plus years in the news and entertainment industry, I was often hired for speaking engagements and motivational coaching sessions. Meanwhile, I became a "go to" motivational coach of sorts in a few of the newsrooms I worked in. I would e-blast inspirational quotes (before that became a social media norm) and orchestrate power lunches. Since I had a passion to encourage and inspire people, I was never at a loss for people willing to receive what I felt compelled to share. Little did I know; I was watering my "seed."

An important key to attaining your dream is to become in tune with the part of you that is a visionary. Having vision means you have the ability to think about or plan for your future with creativity, imagination and wisdom. Vision also brings focus, which is why it is most important to write your dream down and define it concisely. Focus is how you are able to develop strategies to help you unlock your dreams and bring them into manifestation.

I was watching an insightful TED talk featuring Mindfulness expert Andy Puddicombe. He talked about the need to take ten minutes out of every day to do nothing. No texting, no chatting, not eating, just —nothing. This time offers space to mentally step away from the distractions and stresses of daily life and become more present and aware in the now. He also did a demonstration where he juggled balls while he continued his verbal presentation. Andy shared that he was able to this by balancing his focus. If he were to focus too much on what he was going to say (internal dialogue), he would drop the balls. Likewise, if he focused too much on juggling the balls (external action), he wouldn't be able to have the right balance of concentration and meditation needed to continue his fluid verbal presentation.

That demonstration is a great analogy for how you have to approach dream building. You must take time out to think about nothing. Allow your mind to be free from the trappings of "to do" lists and just be. Practicing mindfulness in this way allows your creative faculty to share and present ideas to you that you're usually too busy to entertain.

Focus will be key. Within this book are what I consider power tools. I have used or created them to help me get tangible results. They are tools I continue to use with my clients. One is called *The Purpose Planner*. It allows you to drill into your vision at a deeper level so you can set short and long term goals; determine the *major players* that do, or *can* affect, your success, and lay out the tasks that become the basis for your action plan.

As you focus on the exercises and what you learn about yourself, remember that you don't want to focus so intensely on the work and tasks right in front of you that you lose passion and focus for what you're trying to create outwardly - the dream.

What makes this journey an adventure is the mix of the seen and unseen; the tangible and the intangible. The principles in this book will bring positive results. It's not because I'm so special; it's because laws and principles work the same for everyone. For example, the law of gravity works the same for each of us. Test this by jumping off of a chair. It won't matter who leaps, how they leap or when they leap. Anyone who jumps off of a chair will end up on the floor. The laws and principles proven effective for making dreams a reality can work for you like they've worked me and others. Those are the tangible things I can help you with. Still, there are parts of this process that only YOU can do.

As we prepare to move into discovering your dream, make the commitment to: (Indicate YES with a √)

☐ do the exercises and write out your answers.
(You can't hit a target you can't see.)

☐ move forward with your action plans, even when it makes you uncomfortable.

☐ cultivate a healthy level of expectation and gratitude.

Let's get to work.

DISCOVERING
YOUR DREAM

You may be reading this while reflecting inwardly and thinking, "I don't really have a dream of that magnitude-not one that burns inside me with purpose." Look around at the needs in your immediate world, or even the world at large. What you love can be an indicator of where your talents, skills, gifting and passion are tuned. Meanwhile, what you hate could be an indicator of the areas you could use your skills to meet a need. Discovering your dream starts with mining the wealth of treasure on the inside of you. Your gifts and talents represent abilities. Those abilities help define tasks, career types, and areas of passion. Once you narrow down your skills and talents, read over your list. When you connect the dots in a way that makes sense and clicks for you, you've most likely discovered your dream.

List 5 to 10 things or more that you have an unusual knack for, talents you were born with or learned easily. Perhaps you're very organized, have a calming spirit, or are gifted to make things grow. While there may be differences between strengths, gifts and talents, what may be a gift for one person may be only a strength for someone else. Those differences are not for me to define for you. Use these exercises to form your own definitions and see where the list leads you.

IDENTIFY YOUR GIFTS AND TALENTS

_____

_____

_____

_____

_____

_____

_____

_____

_____

_____

_____

_____

IDENTIFY YOUR STRENGTHS

_____

_____

_____

_____

_____

_____

_____

_____

_____

_____

_____

_____

Another useful tool may be for you to list *where* you use your gifts as well as *how*. You may realize your are limiting yourself in ways you shouldn't. For example, consider why you are using certain gifts and talents in only certain places. Dig as deep as you can.

You may find it a bit difficult to generate this list. If so, you may want to ask people who are close to you and know you well. It can be difficult to identify what's special about ourselves because what we do is such a natural part of us; we don't recognize it for the gift it is. However, these skills and talents stand out tremendously to those around us who have benefitted from what we share and provide. Have no doubt; others appreciate and recognize your unique gifts and skills - even if they don't always verbalize it.

You may also get inspiration for this list by thinking back to the *major players* in your life. If you were fortunate, you may have had a mentor, parent or teacher who recognized a special ability you had. She or he may have reprimanded you for doing something " all the time" or identified something you did as uncommon.

Now, Breathe! Take a moment and notice any uneasy thoughts and feelings you are having now about listing your attributes. Is it hard to celebrate and appreciate you? If yes, why?

Share your thoughts in the "From Dream to Reality" FB Group. Get support and let me know how you're doing!

https://www.facebook.com/groups/1603564546551500/

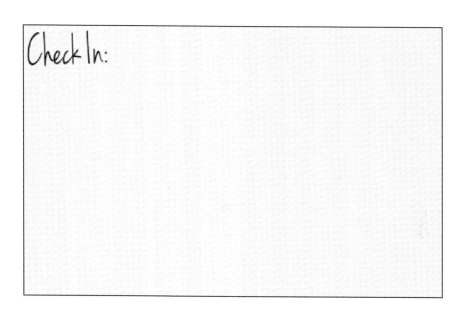

Check In:

As you work through any negative self-talk or limiting beliefs about yourself, remember: everyone has uncommon gifts. Sadly, we seem to appreciate some more than others. For example, social norms will celebrate musical gifts and talents but not those of uncommon teachers. This type of thinking causes many to devalue, under develop and underutilize those types of gifts and skills. For some, their talents and innate abilities often go unrecognized and undeveloped. Another great way to grow through the process is to check in with the "From Dream to Reality" Facebook Group.

Talk with friends, family, even coworkers. I'll bet you become inspired hearing about the things they value in you —things you've taken for granted. You may find that after those conversations you have even more to add to your list.

Once you have completed your list, it's time to filter. Look over each item and make sure it still applies to who you are today. Consider whether you are using your talents and skills in a way that best reflects your *current* set of ideals and beliefs. Are they things that energize you? Are you passionate or motivated by them? If not, let's assess why. It's possible to be proficient in, or good at, something that no longer serves where you are going. For instance, I am a good news anchor but have no desire to serve in that way anymore. I know my calling and purpose is headed in a new direction. If that's the case for you, cross those items off of your list. However, if you know certain gifts and talents *are* a part of what you need for where you're going and still have no passion for them — you'll need to identify *why*. Is it fear? Is it knowing you're not fully developed in an area and need more training? Or is it tied to something deeper, like depression? If so, are you open to having a conversation? Can you talk to a friend? Should you reach out to a coach or therapist? Even taking action in that way is powerful. You can't freely move forward if you're tied to the past. Have the conversation. After all, your dream depends on it.

Let us know if you need help locating a Coach or Therapist. We want you to be healthy, happy and whole as you pursue your path to purpose.

Be truthful. Do you need help?

Yes _____   No _____

https://www.facebook.com/groups/1603564546551500/

Now that you've identified your special skills, talents and gifts, map out how you use what you have! Review your list of skills, strengths, talents and gifts. Use the fields on the following pages to share **how you use each one of those skills**. Be sure to clearly define how you operate in those skills and talents in very practical ways.

How I Currently Use My Skills and Talents

_____

_____

_____

_____

_____

_____

_____

_____

_____

WELL DONE! You've identified your special skills, talents and gifts, and clarified how you use them in practical ways. Now rate them from one to ten. **One (1)** will be the thing you are *most passionate* about and **ten (10)** will be the thing you are least *passionate about.*

Having identified the top three things that really give you excitement or energize you in a way that is most fulfilling, **look for what ties those things together.** Do they have a thread of commonality? Are they, or could they be, interwoven in some way?

For instance, I shared with you how I liked to write stories and had the gift of gab. My friends also say I have the gift of inspiring and encouraging people. I may not have counted that as special before, but when my friends pointed out that I'm the one everyone comes to for advice, I took notice of it. It was no surprise to anyone when I became a journalist, working as a news anchor and reporter. When I left news I moved into entertainment, which enabled me to operate in another area of passion. Now, as a Life Strategist and Mindset Coach, I'm immersed in an even deeper level of my passion. This is the way you will begin to connect your own dots.

Once you've identified how you use those two or three key skills and gifts, **make one last list of how you would most** *like* **to be able to utilize those talents.**

For example, let's say someone is an at-home mom with a passion for teaching and being a caretaker. She may currently be using her skills of listening, providing, teaching and nurturing to raise her own children. However, she may want to use those skills to start an in-home daycare or get a home schooling license. One client took that same set of skills and went back to school to become a nurse after her baby turned two years old. The possibilities are endless! **What is YOUR purpose?** That's the question at the heart of this work.

Some of you may find that you are not using the skills and talents you're most passionate about in *any* area of your life right now. Don't beat yourself up about that. This process is designed to help you locate yourself from dream to reality. If you discover you're "off the map," at least you know where you are, and you can get back on track.

So—focus. Make that last list of how you would most *like* to be able to utilize your dominant talents—the skills you're most passionate about. Challenge yourself to stretch beyond your boundaries of comfort. Think outside of the blah and ordinary. Most importantly, be honest.

I will warn you:

- don't edit your thoughts

- don't worry about how to make it happen

This is key because you don't want to destroy your hopes before you even get your dreams on paper! I have found it insightful to do this self-surveying and excavating each time I enter a new season of my life. I can tell it's a new season because my interests, passions and inspired thoughts draw attention to things I may not have given much thought to before. Often, previous ideas and concepts return to me in new and interesting ways.

There are several tools that can help you finely tune your area of purpose. This following list is inspired by *The Path*, written by Laurie Beth Jones. I've shared how it was a light in a dark tunnel when I needed insight to reposition in my own life. I can't say it enough: her book is a life-changing gem. Add it to your dream-building library!

Ready to drill down even deeper? Take your gifts and talents list and give it pinpoint focus by determining what character traits drive your purpose and what areas of service you're most drawn to. For example, are you a builder or nurturer? Put a star by each category that resonates strongly with an aspect of how you want to share your gifts with the world.

Choose as many categories that apply to you. We'll filter down the list in a bit. Right now, think outside the box; connect with those long lost aspirations. Reach deep, don't restrict yourself, and try to get the thoughts out of your head. Gut reactions are best used here. This allows you to record your thoughts without filtering them through the voice of judgement — yours, or that of those around you.

Facebook Check-In

If you have any questions about the exercises or just want to check in, join me in the FB Group where I am answering question and sharing extra insights.

https://www.facebook.com/groups/1603564546551500/

Did you do this check in?

Yes_____   No_____

Areas of Service

1. Explorer | Visionary
explore, discover, imagine, invent, create

2. Advisor | Nurturer
counsel, develop, help, support

3. Artist | Performer | Writer
express, illustrate, speak, demonstrate

4. Builder | Organizer | Manager
construct, plan, oversee, lead

5. Adventurer | Protector
dare, risk, guard, protect

6. Teacher | Healer
balance, explain, inform, restore

7. Philosopher | Researcher | Journalist
analyze, document, investigate, report

8. Executive | Owner
administer, direct, originate, pioneer

9. Humanitarian | Philanthropist
benefit, contribute, donate, promote

10. Coaches | Counselors | Clergy | Ministers
assist, enlighten, mentor, reveal, uplift

Most people will fit into more than one category. That's not unusual. Many of you are fortunate to have several strengths and innate gifts.

What categories resonated most with you? If you feel more aligned with the category of Coaches, Counselors, and Clergy, you have a hunger to assist, enlighten, mentor, reveal and uplift people in your immediate world and beyond. If your skills and passions are more aligned with the category of the Explorer and Visionary, you thrive in being able to discover, imagine, invent and create. This explains why someone might be more inclined to work as a consultant or therapist in the trenches helping people, and another person makes their great contribution working for an app development company —serving people through products and services they create.

My Top 3 Areas of Service are...

Take a moment. How do you feel? Each level of clarity should infuse you with hope. It's like seeing that little light at the end of the tunnel growing a bit brighter. Don't be surprised if you also feel a little anxious. Breaking through comfort zones and facing the unknown can leave you feeling a little vulnerable. Feel the fear and push forward anyway! Sit. Examine your body, are you tense or relaxed? What are you feeling?

Check In:

You are on a mission, and you're doing great! Your "future you" will thank the "present you" for sticking with the process.

Take a deep breath. You have cleared away some weeds that were covering up that dream seed planted inside of you. You may be thinking about aspirations and desires you buried and thought died long ago. Let your inspired thoughts and inner wisdom lead you.

I believe my purpose
                    has to do with . . .
                        involves . . .
                            is to . . .

For some, writing down what you believe to be your greater purpose will feel like a burden lifted. Others may feel quite indifferent. Some will believe or feel they can't answer the question. No matter where you are along the path remember this: When you are ready - you are ready.

I know this space. There have been two times in my life when I wasn't quite sure in my path to purpose. It was an unsettling part of my journey, but so needed.

When I left the news industry, I had NO idea where I would land. After 15 years as a journalist, I ended my career in news on a Friday and spent all of the following Monday in a closet. I wanted to be in prayer, so I told myself. I also think I couldn't bear seeing the news on any station now feeling like an outsider. WHO am I if I'm not a news anchor anymore?

The path to finding my purpose for the next season of my life unfolded slowly. There were times I felt like I was just swinging at piñatas. Finally, when I quit trying - trying to be what I used to be, trying to be what others thought I should be - I became open to the truth of a new purpose revealing itself in my heart. A new dream seed was planted. A few months after that, I began working at a mega ministry as a producer for a broadcast seen in 1.2 billion homes. I grew from that place, and not only did I survive —I thrived! I was promoted from that position to an Executive level job, giving oversight to the entire media department. Working there fed my spirit and my soul. Little did I know that the dream seed had more fruit to bear. About six months later I got a call from my agent. The DIY network was looking for a host. Soon after, I also took on a season position as a home improvement show host, which also lead to work with HGTV.

I think back to that master bedroom closet and the twelve hours I spent in the dark. I never would have guessed that before the year ended, I would be so blessed as to work in the area of my great passion as a broadcaster and in my calling as a mentor, advocate and encourager. Not only was my soul content, but my bank account got a nice boost too.

If you can relate, and feel like you're stuck in that dark closet, you must choose. You can either shrink back to that place of comfort and safety where you've been stuck for most of your life, or you can make the decision to step into the truth of your life.

Still not ready? Let me tell you about the other time in my life I felt lost. When downsizings were numerous and the economy took a dive in the U.S. beginning at the end of 2007, I was one of the estimated 2,385,000 people to endure the blow.[2] I'll never forget the night before getting the news. I was sitting on the edge of my bed on my laptop and heard a voice whisper to me just as plain as day, "**_Making change is never as difficult as accepting change._**" I knew that was a God inspired quote because I'm not that wise nor poetic. I just wish God had told me I'd walk that out the next morning. God was right. Accepting the change was far more difficult than making the changes necessary after being let go.

Once I released myself from the anxiety of the abrupt move, I once again found myself on an unfamiliar part of the path from dream to reality. This time, I didn't retreat to the closet. I knew that The Great Giver of Dreams (God) would would plant another seed of purpose in my heart. I wanted the soil to be right and ready. So, I made a decision to feel the hurt, be sad, cry it out, let it go and face forward with anticipation and expectancy in June 2007. By August, I was packing my house and moving to Dallas. A new opportunity was on the horizon, and the reality that grew from this dream seed would totally blow my mind.

Now, it's your turn. Read over your list of talents, skills and gifts. See what areas of service you feel most drawn to. Release any and everything that hinders you from believing beyond sight. Trust that you don't have to know the HOW to embrace the WHAT. This is the moment of your truth —own it *(Restating it never hurts.)* *Breathe. Smile. Now write it.*

I believe my purpose

has to do with...

involves....

is to...

You are on a mission and you're doing great! Your "future you" will thank the "present you" for sticking to it. Before you move on to the next chapter, let's take a moment to marinate in gratitude. You've just learned how skillful and gifted you are, and specifically so! Some people go a lifetime never realizing their own worth. Don't compare nor compete with what you believe someone else is or has. Stay present with yourself. Be thankful for who **you** are and what **you are discovering about you.** You are more than enough!

Question: How often do you celebrate <u>progress?</u>

DO IT NOW!

That's ONE thing you be thankful for.

I'm most thankful...

THE
AUTHENTICITY TEST

This chapter could be subtitled, "Keeping it Real." We've arrived at a place on the journey where you have to be most honest with yourself. Now that you have identified what your strengths, talents, gifts and skills are and how you want to use them, it's time to examine your dream. This is an important part of the process, because if you aren't building your authentic dream, with a pure motive, you are starting your journey on a shaky foundation.

Imagine holding your dream up to the bright light of truth for inspection. Like a crystal prism, when we hold our dream up to this light, we should see authentic aspects of ourselves reflected back to us. This will confirm that the dream you will be building is truly the purpose-driven dream created uniquely for you to live out. It is your assignment in the world. The authenticity is important because your dream should be connected to your own distinctive strengths and talents, not the skills and gifts of someone else. It is easy to become inspired by the success or vocation of another and imagine yourself on their path. Still, the answers to *What do I believe?* and *Why am I here?* can only be answered by you discovering and living out YOUR truth. Think of it this way: You can only ever be average at *trying* to be someone else.

"Terry" can attest to that. He became enchanted with the dream of being the next Anthony Robbins after attending a leadership conference. Unfortunately, his skills and talents were not naturally aligned to support that goal. He failed to spend time investigating his motive behind this new passion and dream. He invested two years taking classes and going to seminars aimed at turning him into a motivational speaker and coach. He learned the processes for writing and delivering a compelling message, but the mechanics alone could not help in execution. Though he was a gifted writer, and had superior wisdom for personal problem-solving, he was never able to really connect with people as a public speaker. He was pursuing an honorable vocation, but he was not blessed with the gifts and talents that would help him develop into his perfect self-expression.

Again, a dream that is uniquely yours will line up with the talents, gifts and skills you possess naturally. Our motivational speaker was told he should consider publishing a book based on his speech material. He finally relinquished his desire to stand in front of crowds and be the "rock star" of motivational speaking. As a result, he gained something greater. This gentleman found success as an author of self-help books. When he committed to operating fully in *his* strengths, constant opposition no longer plagued his efforts. His books became tools of enlightenment and encouragement. He found the *calling* tailor-made for him. He pursued that dream and found that success began pursuing *him!*

Does this scenario sound familiar? Maybe you've seen someone living out a dream that inspired you, and somehow an aspect of yourself became enchanted by the prospect of pursuing *their* dream. What you meditate and focus on becomes the object of your desire. As a result, you naturally gravitate toward creating a life after *their* dream model. If your motives are misguided, you'll eventually end up "beating your head against a brick wall."

"Authenticity is a collection of choices that we have to make every day. It's about the choice to show up and be real. The choice to be honest. The choice to let our true selves be seen."

— Brené Brown, *The Gifts of Imperfection:*

Let Go of Who You Think You're Supposed to Be

and Embrace Who You Are

A purpose-driven dream is authentic and real. It reflects the nature of your true self. I always find that so encouraging because **you can't fail at being you!** A purpose-driven dream will also do more than benefit only you, it serves others. Think of it as your *great assignment.*

HERE'S THE AUTHENTICITY TEST: Examine your dream discovery process. If you chose your dream with the motive of only gaining prosperity and recognition for yourself, head back to the beginning of the exercises and begin again. If your dream was assigned to you by well-meaning loved ones, mentors or other influencers in your life and you've accepted it for misguided reasons (out of a deep-rooted sense of obligation, or out of desperation because you haven't known how to go through the discovery process of unboxing your great purpose) you need to go back to the beginning and reconsider. You should be able to answer this question with confidence, **"Why do I do what I do?"**

It's important that you do what YOU were created to do. There's a reason you were given those unique set of skills, talents and passions. Everything has a purpose —including you. Consider this: Our world operates on a system of supply and demand. This means that there exists a solution for our problems. The solutions lie within people operating in their greater purpose.

For instance, do you need a place to live? There are hundreds of people who have finely-tuned skills in the area of construction. Those whose skill-set it is to build homes can look at housing plans, make sense of the diagrams, cut wood and materials to scale and build beautiful, sturdy and dependable homes. Construction workers and builders create the foundations for our communities and cities. The work is tough. It takes brains *and* brawn. Still, they have a passion for the work. Some crave the satisfaction of working with their hands; others live for the gratification of building something out of nothing. Like that builder, you have skills, passions and talents inside of you to help meet a need or solve a problem.

Warning! Don't be surprised if the dream you pursue doesn't utilize your most recognized or celebrated talent. When you are operating in your greater purpose, you will experience perfect peace with the path you've chosen. Who you are, what you stand for and how you operate in your purpose will reflect the truth of you, your passions and the things that are most important to you.

The people who know me as a journalist or TV personality are usually confused when I share my *dream to reality* story. They just simply cannot comprehend why I would turn down two newscasting jobs to work at a small church in Huntsville, Alabama. "You do what?" they ask. I explain that I use my media, marketing and branding skills to support an up and coming ministry team at my mother's church. Meanwhile, I'm working on my own dream by growing my practice as a certified life strategist, author and internationally sought-after speaker and empowerment coach. For those who understand purpose and calling - they get me. For those who only understand success as society describes it —they're disappointed in me and feel sorry for me. They don't see me getting strong roots below the surface. They don't know about the companies and ministries that hire me to do leadership training and coaching or the colleges and universities that consult with me as part of their student retention and academic success initiatives. They don't see the beginning of my greater purpose taking shape. They'll only "get it" when they hear more about what I'm doing on TV. For them that will equal success. That's sad. I'm glad to know and to help you realize that personal fulfillment is never determined by what others believe about you.

I'm thinking now about a friend of mine from college who was a formidable artist. He painted with such emotion and depth that even his abstract work seemed alive. If I was having a stressful day, I would dip into the art studio. As crazy as this will sound, just being around his work, taking in the imagery, the colors and emotions they emitted put me at ease. Our circle of friends and classmates always thought he would pursue art as a career. I certainly imagined him in some big city hosting his own showing at some swanky gallery. After my college days, I began moving from one television market to another and we fell out of touch. A few years ago I returned to my hometown for an extended stay. While grocery shopping, I ran into another college classmate. After quickly catching-up on our own lives he mentioned my dear friend, the artist. Evidently he didn't move to New York or pursue painting as a vocation, though he still enjoys it as an active hobby. Our artist is now a masseur who works out of a shop he and his wife own. She has a salon on one side and he does massages on the other. "He is in heaven, loves his work and does an awesome job. You should go check him out!" As we said goodbye, I finished self-checking a few items and found myself smiling and chuckling. This scenario in no way matched my expectations for what my dear artist could be doing or how he could be living, but he is living a purpose-driven, passion-fueled life.

His story is a great illustration for identifying your passions, aligning them with your strengths and plugging in to your purpose. His underlying devotion was for providing and promoting healing and well-being. He used art as one vehicle of expression for that gift, then found a truly "hands on" vocation that allowed him use that tool to help people in tangible ways. He also pursued passion over the possibility of a bigger paycheck. Passion + Purpose = Peace. Doing what you love and using your talents and gifts in a purposeful way offers a peace and contentment that money just can't match.

Don't get me wrong; money is important. While it isn't *the* most important thing in life, it *affects* most of life's important stuff. Money can buy you things and afford you experiences that will either magnify and enhance what you possess internally or distract you from what's missing.

Now think about your own life and pursuits. Are you full of zeal about what it is you spend your time doing, or are working toward? If not, then ask yourself the next obvious question: **"Why do I do what I do?"**

As you work through this book, you may discover you have multiple dreams. You have to be careful because some are based in fantasy (like how I secretly wanted to trade lives with Oprah for a year). Others can reflect a desire for something we have a passion and even minor skills or talents to support, but still not be the gifts that lead you to your life assignment (like singing was really meant to be an ancillary tools in the work I do in ministry - not my ticket to Broadway.) Of all the dreams we may entertain throughout our lives, the ones that matter are tied to purpose.

Recognizing your greater purpose and identifying your dream can be scary. Remember this: Being YOU will always be more than enough. When family tries to sway you— when friends just don't get it— remember it's not their seed to carry and give birth to; it's yours. And yes, you may have to work at a few different jobs to help fund your vision, it may not come to fruition until your latter years, but there's a reason it still calls to you. Never give up working on your dream.

You've searched your heart, examined your strengths and talents and given your dream some focus. You've held your dream up to the light of truth and examined it. Now, it's time to take this dream "seed" and plant it back into your heart and nurture it with belief. Believing is key!

BELIEVING...
IS BELIEVING!

"Keep your dreams alive. Understand— to achieve anything requires faith and belief in yourself, vision, hard work, determination, and dedication. Remember all things are possible for those who believe."

~Gail Devers

A vital component for developing a dream into reality lies in your ability to believe in it completely. Eliminate the idea that only "seeing is believing." When it comes to manifesting dreams, "believing is believing!" The capacity to believe doesn't always come easily, because it requires us to trust and have faith in things that do not exist yet, as though they do. This is where you have to internalize what I've shared, look at what you learned about yourself, and decide to trust. You must accept and have faith that there is a divine design that supports you operating as your highest self —a place of perfect self-expression. Just like an oak tree is the perfect self-expression of an acorn, you must believe in the "fruit bearing capacity" of the dream on the inside of you.

Here are a few reasons to believe in you and your dream "seed."

- You can only succeed when you are in agreement
  with yourself.

- You've believed in other things and people all of
  your life; now it's time to believe in yourself.

- The fear of trying and failing is nothing compared
  to the lasting pain of quitting on yourself.

I may not be able to believe for you, but I do believe in you and with you. Open your mind and heart in a way they have never been opened before. It doesn't matter what has or has not happened for you in the past, your dream is meant to come true. There is a place that only you can fill. It's something you do in a unique way, as only you can. This is your destiny. Prepare to walk boldly toward it!

If you want to know about the courage to believe in your dream and persist, talk to Elizabeth Gilbert...her splendid memoir *Eat, Pray, Love* was rejected by publishers for more than six years. SIX years! It then went on to reach more than 10 million readers and would later be spun into a movie earning over $204 million dollars worldwide. What kept her going? What inspired her? That is the $204 million-dollar question. So, what inspires you? The answer to this is vital to creating a life that expresses who you truly are.

Gilbert was inspired to make a bold decision to travel for a year. She made this decision in the midst of personal and professional mayhem, but it gave her the inspiration to move forward in her own life—and to write *Eat Pray Love*, which became an inspiration to millions. If you're not familiar with her memoir, it is an engaging account of one woman's commitment to follow her path from dream to reality, without any assurances outside of her commitment to thrive. She dared to connect the dots of her dream, one moment at a time.

"You can't connect the dots looking forward; you can only connect them looking backwards. So you have to trust that the dots will somehow connect in your future. You have to trust in something – your gut, destiny, life, karma, whatever. This approach has never let me down, and it has made all the difference in my life."

Steve Jobs, CEO of Apple and Pixar Animation Studios
Stanford Commencement Speech - June 12, 2005

The next page contains questions to help catapult you even further down the path toward purpose.

1. What do I expect of myself?
2. Where are things too comfortable for me?
3. What is it I need to accept now?

FEED THE SEED
EAT FROM THE SEED

*H*ave you ever watched a time-lapse video of the germination process of a seed? I encourage you to search for it on the internet. Watching what a seed endures in order to grow will help you understand much of your dream building process, and the life cycle of your dream "seed." It will also give you insight into how you must feed and nourish your dream "seed."

Once planted, many seeds first crack open to shed the outer skin or shell. Likewise, when you discover and recognize the dream "seed", you activate its growth process with your faith. Almost immediately, you will seem to experience loss: the loss of friends who don't get what you're doing; the loss of free time, because you're completely consumed with building your dream; and the loss of finances, because some dreams require an immediate move that involves finances (going back to school, etc.). Those are only a few examples.

You may also experience a loss of identity. That was my experience when I ended my career in news. I was shedding the outer shell of being known as a news anchor. For a time, I felt exposed and vulnerable, trying to figure out who I really was since people could no longer define me based on my job and title. When you commit to follow a dream, you do have to calculate the cost.

Check In: What am I ready to let go of in order to pursue my dream?

Once the old way of thinking, the old identity, the old way of believing and operating is shed, it's time to grow roots. Review the germination video again. Once the old is released the seed repositions and grows down into the dirt before growing up to the surface.

Roots represent the foundation of your dream "seed." The roots hold the seed in place. Your focused intention, right motivation and commitment hold your seed in place. A strong foundation represents the work you've done to vet your thoughts, desires and aspirations through the filters of honesty and integrity. A firm foundation also includes a vision-driven, strategic plan to build your dream. For some, the plan means keeping the job you presently hold, in order to fund the dream you are working to grow. For others, the dream requires increased skills, supplementary training, or further education. This can feel like a set-back; but in truth, it's an opportunity to grow in knowledge and confidence.

I first attended Alabama A&M University in the fall of 1983. As I shared, I was afforded the opportunity to work in news during my Junior year. I tried to manage work while attending college, but being a newbie in the news industry required much more of a commitment than I could have ever imagined. I decided to follow that dream of being a news anchor and put school on hold. This isn't a decision I would recommend for everyone, but it was a strategic move for me. I was blessed and fortunate to have several news directors who believed in me and became quite committed to mentoring me and helping me reach my full potential. This was not always the case in the news industry, so I chose to become a student in the newsroom and absorb all I could from those willing to teach me the things I could have never learned in school. I used to feel a bit of conviction for not finishing my degree, but that was only because of the occasional snide remarks I would get about how I "really should have finished up my degree." I don't regret my decision at all. I know it was smart for me to flow in the favor and timely doors that were opened for me. I also know my story has helped others along the path from dream to reality. I am able to release them from the pressure of trying to follow their dreams according to a ten-step template, or by the expectations of the "peanut gallery" in their lives. There *is* a path for each of us to navigate in pursuit of our dreams, but it is never a straight line between the two points, and the paths rarely take the same twists and turns— no matter how similar two dreams may be.

Do you remember what happens next in the germination process? If you watched a video on the subject as I suggested, (I recommend those posted on YouTube by Neil Bromhall. He has documented and taped various types of seeds in the growth process.) you'll see that seeds grow more than one root. For the purpose of our analogy, just know that while you are working to give birth to your dream "seed" you also have to be rooted.

When you understand how to build the foundation on which you'll cultivate your dream, you will not only discover the purpose that's wrapped up in your dream "seed," but you will also become more committed to developing the skills, connections and strategies you'll need to take what you're passionate about and called to do and create a viable service or product that people are willing to compensate you for. This is how you feed from the seed.

I can get paid to do what I love? I can make a living working from my purpose? YES! If Steve Jobs and Steve Wozniak only tinkered with computers in their parents' garages because they just loved building software systems and hardware platforms, they'd be the type of dreamers that float around with their heads in the clouds — self absorbed in their own passions with no thought of how it could serve the world. Still, getting paid for what you're gifted in and passionate about seems counterintuitive to what society teaches us, but there is a formula that can bring focus to this process and help you unlock your dreams in a way that allows you to build a reality that can sustain you mentally, physically, spiritually and fiscally.

I believe one reason people stop following their dreams and pursuing their purpose is because they believe that wanting to be able to make a living doing what you love somehow cheapens the integrity of your calling —the thing you believe you were born to do. I have even had coaching clients share stories of being guilted into offering their skills or services for very little because they couldn't bring themselves to put a price tag on it. Between the guilt of placing a premium on what they love doing and the old adage, "Do what you love and the money will follow," people are confused. Does that saying mean do what you love and don't worry about charging for it because money will fall from the sky? Uh, no. Sadly, in a practical sense that statement doesn't always prove true, and some zealous dreamers have found out the hard way. Meanwhile, I've coached other clients who are successful in business by society's standards, but they have no sense of inner fulfillment. They are stuck, and in some cases tortured, because they believe that in order to find passion or meaning in work, they have to give up everything else. It's not completely their fault for thinking this way. It reflects an archaic work mentality that believes that only if you work really, really hard will you get a really, really good job. Not true. You'll just end up really, really tired.

Likewise, it purports that if you follow your passions and purpose, you will end up poor, frustrated or both. That old work model is reflected in numerous Venn diagrams online.

Look at the model shared on the next page. Are you operating in any of the beliefs outlined there?

WHAT YOU LOVE

HAPPY + POOR

FRUSTRATED + POOR

HAPPY + RICH

WHAT YOU'RE GOOD AT

UNFULFILLED + RICH

WHAT PEOPLE WANT

Finding Your Bliss[3]

There is another model emerging that reflects the most realistic future for businesses in 2020 and beyond. It takes into consideration not only what you love, what you do well and what people want or will pay for. It also considers what the world needs. These are the four pillars of strength that your dream must be built upon and rooted in.

Take a look at my adaptation of another model. There are many ways to operate in your purpose passion, doing what you do well *and* getting paid for it.

Study this model of the purpose equation.[4] Explore the possibilities.

What you love to do + What the world needs = Your mission

What the world needs + What you are paid for = Your vocation

What you are paid for + What you are good at = Your profession

What you are good at + What you love to do = Your passion

Your mission + Your vocation + Your profession + Your passion

=Your purpose

Creating a life that includes both professional success and personal fulfillment requires an honest assessment that considers both our practical needs and soul goals — issues of fulfillment. Jeffrey Katzenberg, the CEO of DreamWorks Animation, is said to have surprised a crowd by suggesting that young people should not follow their dreams, but their skills: "I believe every human being does something great. Follow that thing you're actually really good at and that may become your passion." Taking another look at the *Find your Purpose* diagram, he's suggesting that the joy of doing something well, something the world needs and will pay for, can turn a job into a career.

Another perspective on finding your career / purpose balance comes from a speech Oprah gave to Stanford business school students: "Your real work is to figure out where your power base is and to work on that alignment of your personality, your gifts you have to give, with the real reason why you are here. Align your personality with your purpose, and no one can touch you. There is no greater gift you can give or receive than to honor your calling. It's why you were born. And how you become most truly alive."

What my seasoned readers should understand from this quote is that you are never too old to locate and operate in your place of purpose. As long as you are here, there is an assignment. It may have nothing to do with a paycheck but everything to do with solving problems and pouring into people in order to have a positive impact in your immediate world and, in turn, the world at large. Think: ripple effect. As you touch people and share what you have, they are encouraged, inspired and motivated to find (and operate in) their purpose and to empower those in their reach. I said you're never too old, but the truth is — you're also never too young. We see news headlines all the time about children, youth and young adults making a difference in the world by serving a community, a cause, or raising awareness for a situation and having tremendous impact. The millennials, as we call them, aren't at all afraid to stand up for something. They're also hungry to find their purpose. It's our responsibility to share any and all tools we can to guide them.

Having impact comes from operating in your personal power. Empowerment is simply your control, deliberately exerted. Will power (empowerment) is something you're born with; it is our choice whether or not we operate in it. I remember reading a report by The Association for Prenatal and Perinatal Psychology and Health. It shares that "Infants are capable of integrating complex information from many sources and, with a little help, begin regulating themselves and their environment. They form close relationships, express themselves forcefully, influencing people from the start."[5] Anyone with or around children can confirm this observation! I'm thinking now of my goddaughter who is almost two years old. Joya came into this world operating in a very special gifting. When she was about 4 months old, we started noticing that she would reach for people in order to hug them. Then we realized that, many times, these weren't people she had previous exposure to. We began paying even more attention to her behavior and realized that she seemed to be choosing people who needed the hugs. Even people who might normally seem surly or extremely self-controlled would melt when Joya would reach for them and rest her little head on their shoulders. She was already operating in her purpose as an instrument of love and healing.

"The people who get on in this world are the people who get up and look for the circumstances they want, and, if they can't find them, make them."

– George Bernard Shaw -

Twice in my *dream to reality* journey I turned down jobs that would have utilized my skills, in order to honor my calling. As tempting as they both were, I couldn't accept the positions because I no longer had passion for newscasting, nor did they align with my redefined E.I.E.I.O. personal mission statement. I've shared the events that lead to me leaving the news industry in 2002. Nonetheless, I was offered two news anchor positions after that time. I knew saying *no* to these opportunities was the right thing to do, and ultimately I had peace about the decisions when I made them. Still, I wouldn't be completely honest if I suggested there wasn't any anxiousness or uneasiness during the process.

Both offers came at separate but equally pivotal points in my life. The first offer came after I had been part of a mass downsizing. I was trying to figure out what my next move would be. I wondered if I should start my own consulting business or work for another ministry. This was the another first for me. I was out of work with no prospects and no agent. I was in what I call the "middle place." Some people also refer to this as "the wilderness." Turning down a news anchor position with no prospects was not only a little scary, it seemed to be a very foolish move to those who loved me and were concerned for me. *Sometimes, easing the fears of those you love is a weightier matter than calming your own.*

In each case, I turned down what would have been a bigger paycheck for peace of mind, greater inner fulfillment, contentment and the sense of operating in my greater purpose. I know you're thinking, "So there IS a trade-off— be rich in money or rich in personal fulfillment." That's not at all the experience I lived out. The pay may have been less, but by choosing to take contractor work instead of the first anchor position offered, I was able to do work that

I loved as a media consultant, travel the world, have the flexibility to travel home and spend time with my mother (who at that time was in her late 70's), work flexible hours and use more of my creative faculties. I felt free. I didn't have to wear the armor of suits to work everyday. I was around music all the time (another great passion of mine) and worked with other tremendously talented and creative people in the gospel music industry.

This position seemed to afford me the opportunity to fill up my artistic cup in ways I hadn't been able to for over 12 years. I hadn't realized it, but parts of me, my creative skills and gifts, had been totally underutilized to the point of atrophy. By choosing to accept work based on my personal mission statement, I ended up working with a notable gospel artist and eventually was invited to sing background vocals for a few major events; associate produce and take a role in a film that won honors at the Hollywood Black Film Festival; and take part in a stage play based on the movie. I counted it an extra blessing to have been able to live out these sideline dreams while doing something that I considered my primary calling for that season. These are opportunities that helped breathe new life into me. I also made friends there and memories that will last a lifetime.

The second time I turned down an anchor job, I actually considered going back into news. I didn't feel called to return to journalism; instead, I was concerned about my depleting savings. By this time, it had been four years since I had stepped away from the corporate ministry job into consulting. The contract for that consulting opportunity had ended, and because I had taken a pay cut to pursue that dream, I had pulled on my savings even more. The thought crossed my mind that I could step back into news for a few years just to build up my finances. If I would have had peace about that decision, I would have taken the job. I didn't. The same morning

I received that communication from the news director interested in me, I had already committed to a job at a small church. The funny thing is, I hadn't even applied for the job yet— I just *knew*.

I have been able to utilize my creative faculties to reach, teach and get more youth in touch with their spirituality. I help coordinate and plan ministry-wide events that serve the community, and I'm able to use my creative faculties to executive produce an annual worship event that has become somewhat of a staple for the youth and young adults at our church. I may not be in charge of an international broadcast anymore, but I definitely see the impact of my reach in my immediate world. I also know that being here over the last three years was purposeful beyond the pay. I needed rest. I started in news when I was 21 years old. I hadn't slowed down since. I am also a cancer survivor (or "slayer" as I call myself), and someone who has worked in highly stressful conditions for most of my career. I needed to be in a position that allowed me to replenish myself from a cellular level. I have just enough responsibility to keep me engaged and content; just enough money to keep me satisfied and comfortable. The winds of change are blowing again. I'm still consulting, accepting speaking engagements and a part of two radio shows, but soon it will be time to reposition to into my full time practice as a certified life strategist. Until I get a "release" in my spirit to leave, I'll stay at this little church and serve to the best of my ability. Why share all of this? It's simple. When the dream "seed" sheds the outer shell it's painful. Change rarely comes easy. I've never seen anyone share this pain transparently. Usually, people go off the grid after a major life shift and only reemerge when they've landed on their feet. How can we learn if we never see their struggle in the 'middle place?' The struggle can be more painful when it seems you're struggling alone. I pray my story helps you know you are NOT alone. This place is temporary.

Take another look at the "Find Your Purpose" chart. The following questions are the game-changers for pursuing your purpose.

1. Can you use your talents not to start over, but to start expanding what is possible? How?

2. Which of your current skills can you offer the world, and in what capacities would exercising those skills bring you fulfillment?

3. How can you use those skills in new ways?

PROTECT
THE SEED

"Your work is going to fill a large part of your life, and the only way to be truly satisfied is to do what you believe is great work. And, the only way to do great work is to love what you do. If you haven't found it yet, keep looking. Don't settle. As with all matters of the heart, you'll know when you find it. And, like any great relationship, it just gets better and better as the years roll on. So keep looking until you find it. Don't settle."

~Steve Jobs

*D*on't Settle! Apathy and unbelief can kill your dream. You've worked so hard to harvest your dream from the seed and discover your purpose, you must work equally has hard to protect it. It's precious! Remember, like a real seed it is most vulnerable just after it's been planted. At that point, the kernel hasn't even had time to fully take root in your heart. If you allow anything to attack your seed, it will be uprooted and destroyed.

There will be several obstacles on this journey from dream to reality, but the number one dream killer is FEAR. Fear has often been referred to as the acronym F.E.A.R., which stands for false evidence appearing real. This implies that an obstacle or setback presents itself to you as being more real, or greater than the truth of the situation. This can become confusing, because there are times when what you fear is real and valid.

81

In those cases, you have to feel the fear and find the strength to move forward anyway. For example, a friend was working on her master's degree. In the middle of her two-year term, her father passed away. That was a very real and very devastating blow. Whenever we experience the death of a loved one or some other tragic event, there is a natural process that we all must go through. We have to accept the hurt, adjust to the loss, and heal. This is a very vulnerable time. At every stage of the grieving process you must fight the urge to give up.

Grief is a heavy emotional burden and, if we're not careful, can consume us with so much despair over the current situation that we are then robbed of our hope for the future. As a result, we become paralyzed. This was the case for my friend "Yvonne." The loss of her only living parent left her feeling alone, unprotected, and uncertain. Again, her feelings were very valid. There were many real-life issues that needed to be sorted out and handled. Those were trying times. We loved her through that season of transition and only became acutely concerned when she began to talk about dropping out of school. She had become completely immobilized by her fear.

Yvonne was able to navigate through that difficult season, but it didn't happen overnight. Every day she was marinating in what she had lost and completely fell out of touch with what she still had and what she once wanted. Her depression (and F.E.A.R.) magnified her insecurities and led her to second guess every decision or desire. It took some time, but my friend was able to reconnect with the reasons she wanted to further her education. In the end, she also remembered how much her father supported her efforts and how proud he was of her tenacity to chase her dreams. The "false evidence" in this instance was the belief that moving forward was fruitless and that her future was lost. We have all suffered loss in our lives, some to a greater degree than others. One truth remains: your life goes on. The world as you knew it may be altered drastically. It may be lined with a thousand heartaches, but you fight to keep moving.

As long as you are still here, there is a purpose and design for your life. Feel the fear and move forward. Find strength in friends, family, books, counseling, life coaches and your faith; but keep moving. Fear can be defeated, but only when you show up for the fight.

You may think your own fear is the greatest danger. That's not necessarily true. Think about the joy and exhilaration you felt when you came to the realization of what you were created to do. The natural reaction to something like this is to share that excitement with those closest to you. Many of these people are what I call the major players in your life. These are the people who already have, or could potentially have, a great amount of influence in your life. They could be an employer, spouse, parent, colleague, family member or a friend. I've seen many dreams get stalled after "the reveal." This is when you zealously share your hopes and aspirations and are met with an abundance of fear-based concerns.

There is a built-in mechanism that kicks in when someone we care about tells us they are about to go out on a limb for something. The protector in us jumps up and yells, "STOP! What are you talking about? Where did that come from? You've never even mentioned that desire before! HOW are you going to make that happen? Are you crazy? Look at all the reasons that won't work! You need to rethink this! Are you even sure this is what you really want?" There you are, holding onto this freshly planted tiny seed thinking, "They're right."

Consider this: if they knew you were going to be successful would they stand in your way? No. The truth is you deserve the right to think out your dream and follow the purpose and calling for your life. It cannot be based on others' comfort levels. For this reason, I suggest you examine your life. Evaluate your major players and group them into the following categories:

Blockers

Supporters

Bridge Builders

Key Holders

Blockers are the people who are motivated by their own fear, envy or both. As you increase your capacity to believe in and pursue your dream, you begin bumping up against the fear factor of those close to you. Your moves make them uncomfortable. Their concerns revolve around how your changes will affect them. For this reason, you can never be truly mentored by an insecure person or someone with an inferiority complex. Most blockers see your dream through a filter of fear, which operates like a magnifying glass for perceived dangers and pitfalls. They minimize the importance of your dream and try to talk you out of pursuing it. Of course, there will be some friends and family who will have honest and authentic concern for you. That's a good thing. Their questions are meant to help you think through obstacles and provide perspective outside of your own, and they'll support you. However, *blockers* don't just express their concerns and then step back; they become dream barriers.

Supporters are the people in your life who will stand with you come rain or shine. They may not share the level of faith you have in your dream or even fully understand your dream, but they stand with you minus any judgment. Some may only be able to support you in prayers or encouraging words; others may support you in resources or finances. These people are gems who help cultivate your seed.

Bridge Builders are people who hear your dream and immediately start thinking of people and resources that could help support your efforts. These are the dot connectors. They're always introducing you to key people, arranging strategic meetings, passing along links to important videos or books —all designed to help you succeed.

Key Holders are the people you may find through your *bridge builders* or those you discover along your path. These people *are* the strategic meetings, mentors and teachers who have important keys that unlock coveted information, opportunities and valuable resources. You may have these people in your life now; if not, the *Purpose Planner* exercise coming up will encourage you to foster those types of relationships.

Once you properly identify the people who have an impact in your life, you have to make tough decisions. What will you do if you identify family or friends as blockers? How will you move forward without the approval or support of people who mean so much to you? The hard answer is—you just do. Unfortunately, not everyone will support or back you. Do your best to share the vision with them. Allow them the opportunity to grow with you. If they are unwilling to do so, you will have to decide whether or not unanimous approval is what you need to move forward with fulfilling the call you have on your life.

What you'll discover is that as you move toward your dreams, your tangible results will speak louder than words. Plus, other like-minded supporters will emerge. Your world will open to other dreamers who connect to you through vision. They "get it," and they "get you." No one attains success on their own, though your journey will require that you walk parts of it alone. The path is long and sometimes lonely. Yet, you that great dream inside of you will lead you to create the life you were born for. Isn't that worth the journey?

WAKE UP!

*"The best way to make your dreams
come true is to wake up." ~Paul Valery*

*B*elieving is only the beginning. Stepping out on faith without any calculated action behind it is futile. As I explained before, some people get swept away with excitement when the seed of their dream starts showing signs of promise. Consequently, they jump into action with no real plan for success. "You can plan to fail, if you fail to plan." That's an old adage that still rings true.

Once you've committed to building your dream into reality, it's time to stop dreaming and start working. We've reached the point in the journey where you'll need to invest your time and energy toward organizing your intentions into a strategic action plan. This is what I call the *Purpose Planner.* I designed it for clients who need help pushing past 'stuck.'

The next few pages will guide you through identifying important goals, major players and tasks necessary to form your action plan. This is an exercise that you can pull out through every season of life.

87

You will want to have extra paper on hand so you can make the most of this exercise.

Plan to spend no more than fifteen minutes on the planner. The time limitation is meant to help you to move swiftly and think freely, unhindered by thoughts of doubt or fear. If you spend too much time on it, you may turn what should be a creative, intuitive and invigorating process into a laborious task. **Don't overthink here.** Find a quiet, comfortable place to work. Try to eliminate any potential distractions.

Do not edit your thoughts at this point. Get everything on paper and operate with the perspective that *anything is possible.* Trying to figure out the *how* will sabotage your efforts here. The planner will help you address the *how* when you get to the section for action items.

Check In:

Do you have a hard time believing anything (you genuinely feel led to go after) is attainable? Why?

Let's talk about it. . .
https://www.facebook.com/groups/1603564546551500/

Purpose Planner

3 LISTS x 3 MINUTES = Dream Strategy
completed in UNDER 10 MINUTES!

*Each of the following sections should take you 3 minutes or
LESS to complete. Work purposefully and swiftly,
trusting your own inner wisdom.*
*Do not second-guess yourself. Complete each section and then
go back to look it over and make changes,
if necessary.*

GOALS: On the following pages you will **list three goals** that directly support your dream. Later, when reviewing your list, you may decide to break them down into short term/long term objectives. That's great! Make sure you stay focused. Don't be afraid to "push" yourself!

MAJOR PLAYERS: **People often create a plan without understanding the important role people around them play in their success or failure.** Whether you want to lose weight, change jobs, or start a new endeavor, you have people who will be affected <u>by</u> or <u>will</u> have impact on your goal. Determine who these people are so you can cultivate support for your mission or prepare people who may be adversely affected. In the beginning I advised you to hold your dream close to you and not share. Now that you are convinced of your dream and committed to the journey, it's time to open doors of possibilities through connections.

There are two categories of Major Players:

1. People who make decisions that **have direct impact** on your current status
    (Employer, Spouse, Parents, Children)

2. People who **could have a positive impact** in helping you reach your dreams
    (Mentors, Spouse, Business Colleagues, Coaches, Counselors. Professional Groups, Organizations)

Some major players (like bosses) must be considered as you determine how to follow your "purpose plan" toward fulfilling your dream. You don't want to announce, "I'm sick of my job and have decided to follow my dreams and start my own business." In these cases try to think from a *win-win* perspective. First, be sure of your plan. Next, be willing to negotiate over what the major player (who would be adversely affected) may need to have peace with your new goals.

Develop a list of NEW Major Players.

These are the mentors who are already successful at what you are working to accomplish:

Physical Trainers, Industry Professionals, Financial Planners or **Investors** (successful ones!), **Marriage/ Relationship experts, Professors, Authors,** etc.

In whatever it is YOU want to accomplish, **study** those who are doing it well and **research** how they made it. Then **find ways to have interaction with these people.** Go to seminars. Search the internet for free video content they have shared. Buy their products. Follow their Periscope channels where they share live nuggets of wisdom. **Put yourself "in the room" with great minds and LISTEN. TALK very little.** WHY? **You're not trying to sell yourself to them; you're trying to LEARN FROM THEM. Mouth closed; ears open!**

ACTION ITEMS: You will find that once you've fine-tuned your goals and decided who the major players are that directly impact your decisions and success, your **action items will write themselves.** These may be the calls you need to make or the research required. Perhaps you need to go back to school, sign up for an apprenticeship, webinar, attend seminars, or workshops or work with a coach for some deeper inner assessment. **STAY MOTIVATED** by identifying 3 action items—then get them done. Do three more and get those done. **COMPLETION** speaks volumes and sets the course for your long-term success.

READY! GET YOUR TIMER SET.

THREE MINUTES FOR EACH LIST—GO!

GOALS

LIST GOALS THAT WILL SUPPORT YOUR DREAM

(Ex: Go back to school. Acting Classes. Seminars. Deadline for a manuscript)

A

_____

B

_____

C

_____

MAJOR PLAYERS

LIST THE PERSON(S) WHO CAN DIRECTLY IMPACT GOALS

(Example: Supervisor, Spouse, Best friend , Business partner, Potential Mentors)

A

B

C

ACTION ITEMS

LIST 3 THINGS YOU CAN DO TO COMPLETE YOUR GOALS

(Example: Career Change: research preferred job, network, enhance resume, attend workshops)

A

_____

B

_____

C

_____

TIP : NOW it's time to let key people know what you are working toward. This helps open networking opportunities with associates and friends of friends. **"You have not because you ask not."** The more you surround yourself with and tap into the brain trust of people who have success in the area you are pursuing, the more you learn and grow knowing what to do and what not to do. Opportunities *(and yes even the God given ones)* come through people. So don't isolate yourself. I will balance this statement with some advice: don't be obnoxious when networking. There is a fine line between being passionate and being aggressively obnoxious.

REVIEW

Once you've identified the What, Who and How components for your dream goals, you can easily go back and start augmenting your list of action items. Every month you should work to meet at least three of your dream goals and then set new goals to maintain momentum. It sounds pretty simple, so why haven't more people set a plan in place to set goals and achieve their dreams? Life gets complicated and busy. We end up taking more time to plan what we'll have for lunch than we take to plan our life's path!

Dreams are like a screenshot of the end desire, which fosters inspiration. With that inspiration, you establish "vision." Now, you must understand that it doesn't end there. Making your dreams a reality requires you to wake up, establish a plan, and work that plan. Discovering "what" to do isn't the hard part— follow through is. Now you have the tools to help you identify a tangible plan with tasks to move you closer to your dream every day. Want to take it up another notch? Get an accountability partner or coach to keep you on the path!

How to Fight
the Enemy (*Inner-me*)

"Only as high as I reach can I grow,
Only as far as I seek can I go,
Only as deep as I look can I see,
Only as much as I dream can I be."

~*Karen Ravn*

There is one more dangerous enemy lurking in the shadows. Peering out from behind massive pillars of doubt and unbelief is the greatest giant we'll come up against on the journey from dream to reality— the enemy that is your 'INNER Me.'

This enemy is relentless. He waits until you've committed to your dream, laid your plan, and stepped out on faith to follow through—then he attacks.

This is where some people will quit on their dream. If you give in to any negative self-talk or self-sabotage, you may find yourself absolutely convinced that there is no way for you to make your dreams come true. If you are not convinced to give up on your dream completely, you are in danger of getting trapped in what I call the dream destruction cycle.

The process looks something like this:

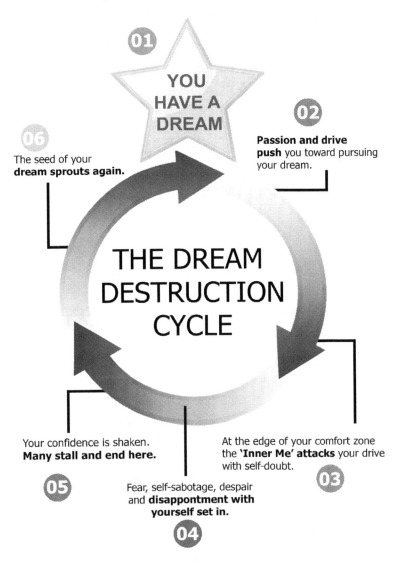

What makes this enemy so hard to fight is that he dwells within you. He has access to your thoughts and emotions, making it even more difficult to put up a fight. Every destructive blow he launches will be fueled with ammunition from your own stockpile of insecurities.

The attack of "Inner me" leaves you feeling belittled. Its motive is to convince you that you're not worthy of your dream. This mindset will remind you of all the reasons you should give up, and most of them will center around areas where you believe you have insufficiencies. They work to discredit your ability to achieve such a big dream.

At these times you have to fight fire with fire. Commit yourself to listening to, watching and meditating on things that promote confidence. You cannot afford to waste any time on frivolous, mindless matters. You have to build yourself up from the inside out. You should attack this negativity like you would a cancer, because in many ways it is. Fear and doubt infect your thinking and can continue to spread until you are emotionally and psychologically paralyzed - in some cases spiritually and physically immobilized—unable to move forward.

Know that every level of achievement comes with a new level of challenge. All dreamers fight the giant of 'Inner Me.' This can be extremely disheartening on the heels of completing your *Purpose Planner* since that exercise awakens your passion and strengthens your hope. However, a good defense rests on a good offense. So prepare your mind for the battle, and rest assured that this is one fight you can win.

Dream builders - if you're looking for accountability - don't forget to post in the *From Dream to Reality* closed group on Facebook. Hopefully, you've been checking in all along, as indicated throughout this book. You can continue to step it up by posting your action items. Take every opportunity to celebrate your progress and encourage others.

Dream Builder Support. . .
https://www.facebook.com/groups/1603564546551500/

Have you shared your dream builder journey with anyone?

Why, or Why Not?

TESTING AND PROVING

"The gem cannot be polished without friction,
nor man perfected without trials."
~Unknown

Until now, most of the work for moving from dream to reality has taken place internally. The dream is planted on the inside of you, and your capacity to believe in the dream is fostered internally. The *Purpose Planner* helped you brainstorm and organize your thoughts, and now it's no longer just a concept — you're moving forward with an action plan to pursue your dream.

You were able to slay the 'Inner Me'; now what are you expecting? Expect the best, but prepare to be tested and tried. No, this is not another evil plot to discourage you. These tests actually help prepare you to be a success!

The tests and trials generally begin after you've started working your action plan and are seeing results. You feel great because you are finally working toward the dream that had only been a hope until now. Then, suddenly, you seem to come to a standstill. Doors that were once frequently opened seem to be shut.

Opportunities no longer present themselves readily, and each day you feel like you're losing momentum. It will seem like some sort of trick, and you'll feel like you've made a terrible mistake. After all, you had the dream, planted it in your heart, nurtured it, announced the dream to those closest to you, fought through the *blockers* and found the *key holders* to help you along the path. *Now*, you're stuck. Nothing seems to work right. You feel as if someone has hit the big pause button on your life. The doom clouds roll in as you begin calculating how you'll save face with family and friends. You lament over the time and money you've wasted, while everything fades to black. Without understanding this season of testing and proving, doubt and fear can rule. At this point, yielding to the process and having a healthy perception is key.

Many believe that, once they commit fully to pursuing their dream, the reward soon follows. They may be prepared for a few challenges along the way, but generally they believe the toughest days are behind them. That's why this season of testing and proving comes as a shock.

Instead of growing through this part of the journey and allowing it to serve its purpose, some will try to push and fight through it on sheer will. I was one of those gals. What I experienced was more frustrating than merely trying to fit the proverbial square peg into a round hole. It was more like swinging a crooked bat at a tiny marble sitting on a stand. No matter how focused I was, or how hard I swung, I missed every time. Eventually, I ran out of steam and fight. Ironically, *that's* when things "clicked." Instead of narrowly focusing on my action items and weekly goals, I started taking inventory of what was happening around me. After working through the obstacles and challenges, I realized I was getting life's version of "on the job training" for the next level of my journey.

Think back to when you first realized your dream. Were you overwhelmed by the prospect of what it entailed? You may have one or more of the following thoughts: *I can't do this; I'm not qualified; I don't have enough experience; I don't have enough money or resources.* You were right. You were no more prepared or equipped to attain or maintain the dream than when you began. That is why trials are so vital. They help perfect the talents, skills and character needed to fulfill your dream. This season also offers you the time and opportunities to acquire provision for your vision. When I came to understand the purpose for the season of "testing and proving," I accepted it as a necessary step along the journey and an indicator that I was moving to the next level toward my goals. When you hit this part of your path, rest assured; this isn't the end. Keep moving!

So the Experts Say...

"Your time is limited, so don't waste it living someone else's life. Don't be trapped by dogma – which is living with the results of other people's thinking. Don't let the noise of other's opinions drown out your own inner voice. And most important, have the courage to follow your heart and intuition. They somehow already know what you truly want to become. Everything else is secondary."
~ Steve Jobs

Experts are important, but they are not always right. Industry experts tend to measure success by formulas—looking back at what is presently working or has worked in the past. Their idea of success is achieved if you can "fit" into a model already proven and tested. If you don't fit, you won't succeed. Again, this is in their limited understanding. The challenge for following your dreams, especially if you're an innovator, is that you have to do it by faith, without the comfort of a formula or a track record of success to lean on. Think about it: if you're creating an app that has never been introduced, you have no idea how it will connect with consumers until you test it and release it. How much more risk was there for the person who first created the concept of apps for smartphones in the first place? Being a dreamer takes a tremendous amount of faith and enthusiasm. Despite your doubts and despite what so-called experts might tell you - if you want the benefits -

you must bear the risk that comes with the honor of being first. This doesn't mean you can't improve your skills and make things better by taking someone's advice, especially that of a proven expert. But sometimes, when someone says you can't do something related to your passion, you have to get up the nerve and do it anyway.

Whether you fail or succeed, what should matter most is that you're doing what you love to do, what you are compelled to do— what you are created to do. It's not always about what you "earn" from it, even though making a living is important. For that reason, there will be seasons of your life when you may have to work in positions that fall outside the realm of your purpose-driven position. And who knows, maybe you will create something that resonates with people simply because they haven't seen it before, read it that way or heard it like that.

Honestly, think about it. It's no real surprise anymore when someone creates the next big thing after being told "No!" by expert after expert initially. Apple icon Steve Jobs was rejected by both Atari and HP. Some would say the experts got that one wrong. I believe that Steve may not have been a good fit for those companies, because he had vision beyond what they could think or imagine. In that case, a person of his level of genius with no latitude to create and explore would eventually feel as if they were held hostage to limited thinking—their potential wasting away. Likewise, Harry Potter fans are horrified to learn their beloved literary series almost never made it into print. J. K. Rowling reportedly went through the submission and rejection process twelve times before finally getting her first book in the series published. I mean REALLY? Who passes on Harry Potter?

Experts are certainly valuable; you need them. When they reject your product, service or idea, you should use their feedback to inspect your work and fix any cracks in the foundation. Modify, improve, test and go again. If you KNOW you have nourished and cultivated the seed of a dream you were supposed to grow, let a "no" drive you to be better. Raise the bar on excellence. See good and go for great. But whatever you do: Don't. Let. Them. Stop. You. Sometimes, even the experts get it wrong. Continue the Journey.

THERE ...
IS HERE

"To dream anything that you want to dream. That's the beauty of the human mind. To do anything that you want to do. That is the strength of the human will. To trust yourself to test your limits. That is the courage to succeed."
~Bernard Edmonds

*P*icture yourself on top of a mountain. Its panoramic views of the surrounding coastline are magnificent. At this moment, you sit enjoying the breathtaking beauty of it all. It's at this place where everything feels perfectly aligned. Tired from the climb, you start to feel the aches and pains of scrambling up footholds, using rocks to pull yourself from ledge to ledge. In fact, until this moment, you had forgotten about how challenging and treacherous the journey has been. Now none of that matters as you rest in the overwhelming sense of peace and fulfillment. You turn to watch the sun setting over the summit and realize you've seen this place before. You are "there." This is your dream. This is where the deepest desire of your heart connects with the passion that burns in you to do what you were created to.

It started with a question: *What are you born to do?* From there —a dream sparked a promise you made to yourself that one day you'd get "there." Congratulations! There ... is here. Oh, I know. You were waiting for a definitive end destination. What you didn't realize is that the dream building process continues from good to better and from better to best. Then, you start all over on another level going from seed to soil, from soil to root and from root to stem - from good to better and best...again! Dream. Believe. Build. Wash and repeat. At each successful level you reach, you'll experience the refreshing thought: "You are there." Enjoy the achievement each and every time.

What a journey. If I had the opportunity, I would love to sit down with each and every one of you, face to face, and ask, *"What would the you of today tell the you from five years ago? How have you grown personally, professionally and spiritually? When you look back, can you see how words and images impacted your thoughts, which, in turn, influenced your decisions and actions? Now that you know how to navigate the journey from dream to reality, how will you use that knowledge?"*

Hearing about your dream, the path you took to achieve it, and how you grew in the process, is what motivates me as I sit, working to complete the manuscript for this book.

What do you do now that you're here - where dream is now reality? First, enjoy the view. You worked hard; you deserve a time of replenishment. Make sure you work as hard at living in your dream as you worked to achieve it. Set high standards for yourself and never forget the responsibility that comes with holding on to what you've worked for.

Secondly, look back down the mountain. Who do you see climbing up behind you? Part of the responsibility you assume once you realize your dream is to help someone else make their dream come true. Whether you take on the role of encourager or financier, show thanks for the assistance you got along the journey by being a *bridge- builder* or *key holder* for someone else.

I don't know your name or where you are in the world reading this right now, yet still—we are connected. We are connected by the desire to do something meaningful with our lives for the benefit of others as well as ourselves. We are connected by a passion to search and find the answers we need to unlock our destiny. Finally, we are connected by hope.

Dreamers are often criticized and thought of as flaky or weak-minded. We know that is not the case. In fact, that's why I included quotes about dreams and dreaming shared by powerful people from various arenas of life. I wanted to constantly inspire you along the journey so you would believe, beyond a shadow of a doubt, that to dream is powerful and to live the dream is courageous. Every great achievement began with the seed of a dream.

I invite you to share this book or another copy with those who are stuck on the path between dream and reality. Share your insights as well. Share your journey from dream to reality with **me**. As I've shared pieces of my journey to inspire you, I know your journey will inspire me.

ABOUT THE AUTHOR

Janette R. Smith is a compassionate and fiery certified change agent, and keynote speaker most sought after for being able to help clients "push past stuck." Janette's presentation style incorporates her vast experience as an Emmy, Telly and Aurora award-winning journalist of 25 plus years in the broadcast industry. While working as an anchor, reporter and show host in Cincinnati, Dallas, and Atlanta, she fulfilled a wide range of dreams including: beating cancer; riding a bull (for 2.7 seconds); living at sea on the aircraft carrier USS John C. Stennis; singing live with Grammy, Dove and multi-platinum gospel artist Fred Hammond; and working on a promotional campaign with Oprah.

Once Janette fulfilled her desire to work in broadcast news, she followed another dream to work in the entertainment industry. For five years she served as host for *Ask DIY* - a syndicated home improvement show for the D.I.Y. Network - and hosted specials on HGTV.

Having grown up as the daughter of a United States Air Force Lt. Colonel, Janette developed a strong desire to make a difference in the lives of people from all cultures and all walks of life. As a result, Janette spent six years traveling the world producing human interest stories for Creflo Dollar Ministries while heading up its media department as Executive Producer.

Janette is currently an SI *(Strategic Intervention)* Certified Life Strategist & Executive Coach, TV Personality, Radio Host and PeriCoach on Periscope (#Peri10k, #TagTribes).

ENDNOTES

[1] Oprah Winfrey (2009) Defining Destiny: What I Know For Sure. *O, The Oprah Magazine,* November 2009. Retrieved from: http://www.oprah.com/omagazine/What-Oprah-Knows-for-Sure-About-Destiny#ixzz3lVE2r024

[2] "Job Losses Caused by the Great Recession." Wikipedia. Web. Accessed October 1, 2015 https://en.wikipedia.org/wiki/Job_losses_caused_by_the_Great_Recession

[3] "Art by Venn Diagrams." Muddy Colors. October 3, 2013. Accessed August 10, 2015. *I am unable to credit where the following infographic content originated. I tried, but photo snatching has obliterated the original credits.* http://muddycolors.blogspot.com/2013/10/art-by-venn-diagrams.html

[4] "Find Your Purpose." Laughlin Out Loud Blog. August 21, 2014. Accessed September 1, 2015. http://blog.laughlin.com/2014/08/21/find-your-purpose/

[5] B. Chamberlain, Ph.D., David. "Babies Remember Birth." Birthpsychology.com. May 12, 2013. Accessed October 11, 2014. https://birthpsychology.com/sites/default/files/pdf/babies-remember-birth.pdf.

Made in the USA
Middletown, DE
04 August 2017